HUMAN RESOURCE MANAGEMENT

:: Author ::

GANESHBHAI C. NARBHAVAR

(M.COM., B.ED., G-SET)

PUBLISHED BY

Hemchandracharya International Publishing House
HQ. At & Po. Chaveli., Ta- Chansma,
Dist- Patan, North Gujarat, India, Asia.
www.iphouseindia.com

First Publication: 25TH JANUARY, 2015

Copyright: Author

(c) **GANESHBHAI C. NARBHAVAR**

ISBN:- 978-15-08712-15-2

Price: Rs.750/- INDIA
        $ 15 OUTSIDE INDIA

PUBLISHED BY

Hemchandracharya International Publishing House
HQ. At & Po. Chaveli., Ta- Chansma,
Dist- Patan, North Gujarat, India, Asia.
www.iphouseindia.com

Dedicated
to
my
Parents

An Overview of Contents

- **Human Resource Management (HRM) - Definition and Concept**
- **What is Human Resource Planning ?**

- **The Changing Role of the HR Function**
- **Typical Functions of a Human Resource Manager**

- **Staffing Role of the HR Manager: Strategic Workforce Planning**

- **Talent Management by Successful Companies**
- **Performance Management as a HR Management concept**
- **Strategic Human Resource Management - A Tool to Achieve Organizational Goals**
- **Managing Employee Performance**
- **Managing Employee Relations**

- **Diversity in Organizations**

- **Managing Workforce Diversity**
- **An Online Guide to OSHA Safety Regulations, Standards and Checklist**
- **Human Resource Audit - Meaning, Phases and its Advantages**

- **Some Strategies for fresh graduates**

- **The Challenges of Managing Attrition in Contemporary Organizations**

Human Resource Management (HRM) - Definition and Concept

We often hear the term Human Resource Management, Employee Relations and Personnel Management used in the popular press as well as by Industry experts. Whenever we hear these terms, we conjure images of efficient managers busily going about their work in glitzy offices. we look at the question "what is HRM ?" by giving a broad overview of the topic and introducing the readers to the practice of HRM in contemporary organizations. Though as with all popular perceptions, the above imagery has some validity, the fact remains that there is much more to the field of HRM and despite popular depictions of the same, the "art and science" of HRM is indeed complex. We have chosen the term "art and science" as HRM is both the art of managing people by recourse to creative and innovative approaches; it is a science as well because of the precision and rigorous application of theory that is required.

As outlined above, the process of defining HRM leads us to two different definitions. **The first definition of HRM is that it is the process of managing people in organizations in a structured and thorough manner.** This covers the fields of staffing (hiring people), retention of people, pay and perks setting and management, performance management, change management and taking care of exits from the company to round off the activities. This is the traditional definition of HRM which leads some experts to define it as a modern version of the Personnel Management function that was used earlier.

The second definition of HRM encompasses the management of people in organizations from a macro perspective i.e. managing people in the form of a collective relationship between management and employees. This approach focuses on the objectives and outcomes of the HRM function. What this means is that the HR function in contemporary organizations is concerned with the notions of people enabling, people development and a focus on making the "employment relationship" fulfilling for both the management and employees.

These definitions emphasize the difference between Personnel Management as defined in the second paragraph and human resource management as described in the third paragraph. To put it in one sentence, **personnel management is essentially "workforce" centered whereas human resource management is "resource" centered**. The key difference is HRM in recent times is about fulfilling management objectives of providing and deploying people and a greater emphasis on planning, monitoring and control.

Whatever the definition we use the answer to the question as to "what is HRM?" is that it is all about people in organizations. No wonder that some MNC's (Multinationals) call the HR managers as People Managers, People Enablers and the practice as people management. In the 21st century organizations, the HR manager or the people manager is no longer seen as someone who takes care of the activities described in the traditional way. In fact, most organizations have different departments dealing with Staffing, Payroll, and Retention etc. Instead, the HR manager is responsible for managing employee expectations vis-à-vis the management objectives and reconciling both to ensure employee fulfillment and realization of management objectives.

Importance of HRM for Organizational Success

We have discussed the basic concept of HRM and the ways in which it helps the organization meet its goals. we discuss the reasons for organizations to have a HRM strategy as well as the business drivers that make the strategy imperative for organizational success. It is a fact that to thrive in the chaotic and turbulent business environment, firms need to constantly innovate and be "ahead of the curve" in terms of business practices and strategies. It is from this motivation to be at the top of the pack that HRM becomes a valuable tool for management to ensure success.

The Evolving Business Paradigm

One of the factors behind organizations giving a lot of attention to their people is the nature of the firms in the current business environment. Given the fact that there has been a steady movement towards an economy based on services, it becomes important for firms engaged in the service sector to keep their employees motivated and productive. Even in the manufacturing and the traditional sectors, the need to remain competitive has meant that firms in these sectors deploy strategies that make effective use of their resources. This changed business landscape has come about as a result of a paradigm shift in the way businesses and firms view their employees as more than just resources and instead adopt a "people first" approach.

Strategic Management and HRM

As discussed on modern day HRM practices, there is a need to align organizational goals with that of the HR strategy to ensure that there is alignment of the people policies with that of the management objectives. This means that the HR department can no longer be viewed as an appendage of the firm but instead is a vital organ in ensuring organizational success. The aims of strategic management are to provide the organization with a sense of direction and a feeling of purpose. The days when the HR manager was concerned with administrative duties is over and the current HRM practices in many industries are taken as seriously as say, the marketing and production functions.

Importance of HRM for Organizational Success

The practice of HRM must be viewed through the prism of overall strategic goals for the organization instead of a standalone tint that takes a unit based or a micro approach. The idea here is to adopt a holistic perspective towards HRM that ensures that there are no piecemeal strategies and the

HRM policy enmeshes itself fully with those of the organizational goals. For instance, if the training needs of the employees are simply met with perfunctory trainings on omnibus topics, the firm stands to lose not only from the time that the employees spend in training but also a loss of direction. Hence, the organization that takes its HRM policies seriously will ensure that training is based on focused and topical methods.

In conclusion, the practice of HRM needs to be integrated with the overall strategy to ensure effective use of people and provide better returns to the organizations in terms of ROI (Return on Investment) for every rupee or dollar spent on them. Unless the HRM practice is designed in this way, the firms stand to lose from not utilizing people fully. And this does not bode well for the success of the organization.

Scope of Human Resource Management

Human resources are undoubtedly the key resources in an organization, the easiest and the most difficult to manage! The objectives of the HRM span right from the manpower needs assessment to management and retention of the same. To this effect Human resource management is responsible for effective designing and implementation of various policies, procedures and programs. It is all about developing and managing knowledge, skills, creativity, aptitude and talent and using them optimally.

Human Resource Management is not just limited to manage and optimally exploit human intellect. It also focuses on managing physical and emotional capital of employees. Considering the intricacies involved, the scope of HRM is widening with every passing day. It covers but is not limited to HR planning, hiring (recruitment and selection), training and development, payroll management, rewards and recognitions, Industrial relations, grievance handling, legal procedures etc. In other words, we can say that it's about developing and managing harmonious relationships at workplace and striking a balance between organizational goals and individual goals.

The scope of HRM is extensive and far-reaching. Therefore, it is very difficult to define it concisely. However, we may classify the same under following heads:

- **HRM in Personnel Management:** This is typically direct manpower management that involves manpower planning, hiring (recruitment and selection), training and development, induction and orientation, transfer, promotion, compensation, layoff and retrenchment, employee productivity. The overall objective here is to ascertain individual growth, development and effectiveness which indirectly contribute to organizational development.

  It also includes performance appraisal, developing new skills, disbursement of wages, incentives, allowances, traveling policies and procedures and other related courses of actions.

- **HRM in Employee Welfare:** This particular aspect of HRM deals with working conditions and amenities at workplace. This includes a wide array of responsibilities and services such as safety services, health services, welfare funds, social security and medical services. It also covers appointment of safety officers, making the environment worth working, eliminating workplace hazards, support by top management, job safety, safeguarding machinery, cleanliness, proper ventilation and lighting, sanitation, medical care, sickness benefits, employment injury benefits, personal injury benefits, maternity benefits, unemployment benefits and family benefits.

It also relates to supervision, employee counseling, establishing harmonious relationships with employees, education and training. Employee welfare is about determining employees' real needs and fulfilling them with active participation of both management and employees. In addition to this, it also takes care of canteen facilities, crèches, rest and lunch rooms, housing, transport, medical assistance, education, health and safety, recreation facilities, etc.

- **HRM in Industrial Relations:** Since it is a highly sensitive area, it needs careful interactions with labor or employee unions, addressing their grievances and settling the disputes effectively in order to maintain peace and harmony in the organization. It is the art and science of understanding the employment (union-management) relations, joint consultation, disciplinary procedures, solving problems with mutual efforts, understanding human behavior and maintaining work relations, collective bargaining and settlement of disputes.

The main aim is to safeguarding the interest of employees by securing the highest level of understanding to the extent that does not leave a negative impact on organization. It is about establishing, growing and promoting industrial democracy to safeguard the interests of both employees and management.

The scope of HRM is extremely wide, thus, can not be written concisely. However, for the sake of convenience and developing understanding about the subject, we divide it in three categories mentioned above.

Processes in Human Resource Management

Each organization works towards the realization of one vision. The same is achieved by formulation of certain strategies and execution of the same, which is done by the HR department. At the base of this strategy formulation lie various processes and the effectiveness of the former lies in the meticulous design of these processes. But what exactly are and entails these processes? Let's read further and explore.

The following are the various HR processes:

1. Human resource planning (Recruitment, Selecting, Hiring, Training, Induction, Orientation, Evaluation, Promotion and Layoff).
2. Employee remuneration and Benefits Administration
3. Performance Management.
4. Employee Relations.

The efficient designing of these processes apart from other things depends upon the degree of correspondence of each of these. This means that each process is subservient to other. You start from Human resource Planning and there is a continual value addition at each step. To exemplify, the PMS (performance Management System) of an organization like Infosys would different from an organization like Walmart. Lets study each process separately.

Human Resource Planning: Generally, we consider Human Resource Planning as the process of people forecasting. Right but incomplete! It also involves the processes of Evaluation, Promotion and Layoff.

- **Recruitment:** It aims at attracting applicants that match a certain Job criteria.
- **Selection:** The next level of filtration. Aims at short listing candidates who are the nearest match in

terms qualifications, expertise and potential for a certain job.

- **Hiring:** Deciding upon the final candidate who gets the job.
- **Training and Development:** Those processes that work on an employee onboard for his skills and abilities upgradation.

Employee Remuneration and Benefits Administration:

The process involves deciding upon salaries and wages, Incentives, Fringe Benefits and Perquisites etc. Money is the prime motivator in any job and therefore the importance of this process. Performing employees seek raises, better salaries and bonuses.

Performance Management: It is meant to help the organization train, motivate and reward workers. It is also meant to ensure that the organizational goals are met with efficiency. The process not only includes the employees but can also be for a department, product, service or customer process; all towards enhancing or adding value to them.

Nowadays there is an automated performance management system (PMS) that carries all the information to help managers evaluate the performance of the employees and assess them accordingly on their training and development needs.

Employee Relations: Employee retention is a nuisance with organizations especially in industries that are hugely competitive in nature. Though there are myriad factors that motivate an individual to stick to or leave an organization, but certainly few are under our control.

Employee relations include Labor Law and Relations, Working Environment, Employee heath and safety, Employee- Employee conflict management, Employee-Employee Conflict Management, Quality of Work Life, Workers Compensation, Employee Wellness and assistance programs, Counseling for occupational stress. All these are critical to employee retention apart from the money which is only a hygiene factor.

All processes are integral to the survival and success of HR strategies and no single process can work in isolation; there has to be a high level of conformity and cohesiveness between the same.

What is Human Resource Planning ?

Human Resource Planning (HRP) is the process of forecasting the future human resource requirements of the organization and determining as to how the existing human resource capacity of the organization can be utilized to fulfill these requirements. It, thus, focuses on the basic economic concept of demand and supply in context to the human resource capacity of the organization.

It is the HRP process which helps the management of the organization in meeting the future demand of human resource in the organization with the supply of the appropriate people in appropriate numbers at the appropriate time and place. Further, it is only after proper analysis of the HR requirements can the process of recruitment and selection be initiated by the management. Also, HRP is essential in successfully achieving the strategies and objectives of organization. In fact, with the element of strategies and long term objectives of the organization being widely associated with human resource planning these days, HR Planning has now became Strategic HR Planning.

Though, HR Planning may sound quite simple a process of managing the numbers in terms of human resource requirement of the organization, yet, the actual activity may involve the HR manager to face many roadblocks owing to the effect of the current workforce in the organization, pressure to meet the business objectives and prevailing workforce market condition. HR Planning, thus, help the organization in many ways as follows:

- HR managers are in a stage of anticipating the workforce requirements rather than getting surprised by the change of events
- Prevent the business from falling into the trap of shifting workforce market, a common concern among all industries and sectors

- Work proactively as the expansion in the workforce market is not always in conjunction with the workforce requirement of the organization in terms of professional experience, talent needs, skills, etc.
- Organizations in growth phase may face the challenge of meeting the need for critical set of skills, competencies and talent to meet their strategic objectives so they can stand well-prepared to meet the HR needs
- Considering the organizational goals, HR Planning allows the identification, selection and development of required talent or competency within the organization.

It is, therefore, suitable on the part of the organization to opt for HR Planning to prevent any unnecessary hurdles in its workforce needs. An HR Consulting Firm can provide the organization with a comprehensive HR assessment and planning to meet its future requirements in the most cost-effective and timely manner.

An HR Planning process simply involves the following four broad steps:

- **Current HR Supply:** Assessment of the current human resource availability in the organization is the foremost step in HR Planning. It includes a comprehensive study of the human resource strength of the organization in terms of numbers, skills, talents, competencies, qualifications, experience, age, tenures, performance ratings, designations, grades, compensations, benefits, etc. At this stage, the consultants may conduct extensive interviews with the managers to understand the critical HR issues they face and workforce capabilities they consider basic or crucial for various business processes.

- **Future HR Demand:** Analysis of the future workforce requirements of the business is the second step in HR Planning. All the known HR variables like attrition, lay-offs, foreseeable vacancies, retirements, promotions, pre-set transfers, etc. are taken into consideration while determining future HR demand. Further, certain unknown workforce variables like competitive factors, resignations, abrupt transfers or dismissals are also included in the scope of analysis.

- **Demand Forecast:** Next step is to match the current supply with the future demand of HR, and create a demand forecast. Here, it is also essential to understand the business strategy and objectives in the long run so that the workforce demand forecast is such that it is aligned to the organizational goals.

- **HR Sourcing Strategy and Implementation:** After reviewing the gaps in the HR supply and demand, the HR Consulting Firm develops plans to meet these gaps as per the demand forecast created by them. This may include conducting communication programs with employees, relocation, talent acquisition, recruitment and outsourcing, talent management, training and coaching, and revision of policies. The plans are, then, implemented taking into confidence the mangers so as to make the process of execution smooth and efficient. Here, it is important to note that all the regulatory and legal compliances are being followed by the consultants to prevent any untoward situation coming from the employees.

Hence, a properly conducted process of HR Planning by an HR Consulting Firm helps the organization in meeting its goals and objectives in timely manner with the right HR strength in action.

The HRM Function and its Role in Organizational Processes

The Changing Role of the HR Function

Of all the support functions, the HRM (Human Resource Management) function is a critical component of any organization. Apart from finance, which serves as the lifeblood of the organizational support functions, the HRM function more than any other support function, has the task of

ensuring that the organizational policies and procedures are implemented and any grievances of the employees are taken care of. For instance, it is common for the HRM function in many organizations to combine hiring, training, providing assistance during appraisals, mentoring employees, and deciding on pay structures and grades. This means that the HRM function has its task cut out wherein it has to take care of the "people" side of the organizational processes.

Considering the fact that the ascent of the services sector (IT, Financial Services, BPO) has meant that people are the key assets for organizations, the importance of the HRM function has grown by leaps and bounds thanks to the preponderance of the services sector. This has given impetus to many aspiring HR professionals to try and make a career for themselves in the HR field thanks to the burgeoning demand for HR professionals.

Change in Conception from Reactive to Proactive

Many people think of the HR manager as someone who attends to complaints from employees, appears at the time of appraisals, and generally is useful only when there is a genuine need for him or her. This is the classic old world thinking wherein HR managers were confined to these activities alone. The reason for such conceptions is that most of us are used to our parents and other older generation people referring to HR managers as labor officers whose sole function is to take care of payroll and disputes. However, times have changed and in the recent decades, the **HR function has emerged as a key function in itself wherein the HR professionals are proactive and preemptive in nature**. What this means is that HR managers anticipate the crises and preempt them from happening instead of waiting for the crisis to appear and then resolve it. Further, unlike in earlier generations where there were chances of strikes and lockouts of the organizations in the manufacturing sector, the services sector does not have any place for these and hence, the role of the HR professionals have evolved to a point where they have moved from reactive mode to proactive mode. This means that in many multinationals, the HR professionals regularly have what are known as one-on-ones or individual meetings with the staff to try and understand their grievances, seek feedback, and overall focus on how to prevent any kind of crisis from happening.

The HR Professionals and Demand for HR courses

Indeed, apart from hiring, training, and payroll, which still have lot of importance to the HRM, function, the addition of the activities mentioned above has lent a touch of glamour to the otherwise staid and dull profession. It is no wonder that in institutes like XLRI have seen a surge in demand for their courses in HR. Moreover, even in other management institutes, there is an increase in the number of graduates who are choosing HR as their specialization. All these trends point to the conclusion that the HR profession is now well sought after and something that is not relegated to the sidelines.

HR Professionals Have Fun as Well

The changing role of the HRM function is especially visible in the IT and BPO sector where they are also engaged in organizing offsite events, which are held in a resort or in a hotel and which provide the employees with a chance to brainstorm about issues in a relaxed and slow manner outside of the confines of the office. This trend has made the HRM function very busy because a lot of planning goes into organizing these events and indeed, in multinationals like Fidelity, this is now handled by dedicated HR staff apart from the regular staff.

Typical Functions of a Human Resource Manager

Introduction: The Typical Functions of a HR Manager

Until now, we have discussed how the HRM function in organizations works and the role of the function in organizational processes. We have also discussed the changing nature of the HRM function in recent years and how with the introduction of enterprise software, an entirely new dimension has been added to these functions. **This discusses the typical functions of a HR manager and analyzes how he or she can make a positive contribution to the organization and add value to the process**. First, the HR manager has to juggle between hiring, training, appraisals, and payroll among other things. This means that a typical function of the HR manager would encompass the end to end management of the employee people lifecycle which means that the HR manager would have to take care of everything that is concerned with the people aspect right from the time the employee enters the organization till the time the employee quits or retires from the organization. Hence, the lifecycle of an employee's time in an organization has to be managed and this means that the HR manager is responsible for the hiring, training, appraisals, payroll, and exit interviews.

Entry to Exit: Managing the Employee Lifecycle

If we take each of these activities in turn, we find that hiring is done in conjunction with the line managers who put out their requirements periodically on the kind of recruits they want and the number of recruits they want. Once the request reaches the HR manager, he or she has to scour the market for potential recruits. Usually, the HR manager does not personally do this and outsources this function to a placement consultancy. The next step is the interview stage after the shortlists are done and this is an activity where the HR manager either delegates the task of assessing the potential recruits to the staffing team or does the job personally. In large organizations like Fidelity and Microsoft, there are dedicated teams for each of these activities and this is something we would be discussing in detail in subsequent After the interview stage is over, the important task of fixing the salary and benefits of the successful candidates has to be done. This is usually the time when the HR manager plays a critical role as he or she has to determine the fit between the role and the candidate and decide on the quantum of salary and benefits that is appropriate to the role and after examining the budgets for the same.

The Appraisal Process and the Exit Interviews

After these activities, the HR manager is also involved in conducting the last stage of appraisals or evaluating the appraisals. In recent years, the trend is more towards the latter where the HR manager in charge of the business unit evaluates the appraisals instead of participating in the process directly. This is done in a manner to determine the quantum of pay hike or bonuses keeping in mind the same principles that were discussed in the hiring activity. What this means is that the HR manager has to work closely with the line managers to get this done. In many organizations, employees can take their grievances to the HR managers in case they are not satisfied with their pay hikes or the quantum of benefits. They can also complain against their managers in a confidential and private manner. The last activity that the HR manager is involved in is conducting the exit interviews when employees leave the organizations. This is usually done on the last day of the employee's stay in the organization and this process consist of a free and frank discussion on what the employee feels about the organization and why he or she is leaving the organization. The exit interviews offer valuable sources of insights into organizational behavior as the employees can vent their feelings on what works and what does not work in organizations.

Staffing Role of the HR Manager: Strategic Workforce Planning

Staffing and Recruiting during the Boom Years

One of the key areas that the HRM unit works with is the staffing function. Hiring and on boarding of employees' remains a critical activity that many HR managers are yet to master. This is mainly because of the unevenness of the demand and supply in the market for talent. For instance, during the heady years of the IT boom in the early years of the last decade, it was common for many division heads and line managers to walk into the HR manager's office and give him or her target of employees to be recruited over the next three months in the quarter. In the US, the situation was that many HR managers were asked to take in as many H1B or temporary workers to the country on board to meet the critical shortage in staff. In Asia, because of this very reason where many techies had headed to the US and Europe, hiring became a challenge for even the most seasoned HR professionals. The implications for the HR manager are many as his or her appraisal depends on a number of targets including how many they have recruited over the last quarter or the year.

Strategies to Deal with Shortage of Talent during the Boom Years

The way to deal with such a situation was to ensure that the number of people being taken in was based on current and future demand scenarios and identify gaps and surpluses in key skill sets. For instance, in the US, the shortage of those with Java skills was so huge that anyone with an elementary knowledge of the skill was immediately taken in the companies. This meant that the HR unit was simply filling up positions without any strategic planning. Hence, many organizations realized that hiring people without the requisite skills just to fill up positions would do more harm than good to the companies and hence, a conscious decision was taken by the HR managers in conjunction with the line managers to have forecasts of how many employees they would need over a quarter. The point here is that the constant bickering between the HR managers and the line managers took a toll on organizational efficiency and hence, this compromise was arrived at wherein the demand for specific skill sets had to be forecasted by the line managers and the HR managers would then deal with hiring accordingly. The third aspect of the staffing and hiring activity is that many HR managers during the boom years advised the line managers to find employees from other divisions who wanted a change in their job profiles and roles. This internal filling up of positions by inter-division and intra company movement was effective in many companies like Fidelity. Further, overtime by key resources and hiring temporary workers were the norm in many companies. Of course, the overtime work was adequately compensated and employees who were doing so were given additional benefits.

Staffing Strategies during the Ongoing Recession

With the boom years over, the HR managers in recent years are breathing easy as they no longer have to run around trying to meet recruitment targets. Of course, the current challenge before the HR managers to manage the downturn and smoothen the downsizing underway in many organizations. To ensure these objectives in these economically harsh times, HR managers are resorting to passive measures as the first line of action wherein they indicate to the employees that they are on PIP or Performance Improvement Plans and this usually results in natural attrition. Next, instead of downsizing, the HR managers are reducing recruitment so that they do not have to fire employees and instead, these employees can be accommodated elsewhere in the organization. These are some of the aspects of the strategic workplace planning within the hiring and staffing activity that some respected companies follow.

Role of Human Resource Management (HRM) in Leadership Development

Leadership Development in Successful Companies

We have discussed how the HRM function is now seen as a critical and crucial component of the organizational support functions. In particular, we have analyzed how effective people management goes a long way in ensuring better economic performance. Among the components of people, management that the HRM function does is the aspect related to leadership development. Research

into the HRM practices of successful companies has shown that these companies significantly outperform their peers in terms of economic profitability by following the leadership development practices discussed in this. By successful companies, we mean those companies in the Fortune 100 list that have managed to retain their position in the firms over a decade. To put this in perspective, it needs to be remembered that many companies that were in the Fortune 100 list for a few years failed to retain their positions in subsequent years and hence, the fact that these companies have managed to stay in the hunt means that they have outperformed their peers and competitors.

The Components of Leadership Development

The leadership development programs in these companies follow the philosophy of grounding them in value, the expected contributions from the leaders are defined, and the organizational culture geared towards inspiring leaders. Next, the performance management system in these companies is tied to the company's business strategy and it includes talent development activities and leadership objectives that are articulated clearly and succinctly. In other words, promotions are based on individual performance as well as people development activities and these in turn are linked to the business strategy and objectives. These companies also have a leadership pipeline, which means that the leadership development is embedded in their strategic workforce planning which is comprehensive, and longer term oriented. These companies also ensure that they divide their workforce into job families and the potential leaders are identified and groomed for higher roles and responsibilities. In many of these companies, it is common to find lists of potential leaders known as high potentials who are earmarked for fast track career progression based on the organizational assessment of the skills and capabilities of these leaders. Further, the recruitment and training of new employees is based on longer-term analysis of demand and supply patterns, which ensure that newer generation of leaders, are hired into the company to replace those who have made it to the higher levels.

Collaboration between the HRM Function and Senior Management

The HRM functions in these companies work on a collaborative model with their potential leaders which means that the job of people development is not left to the HRM function or the leaders alone. Instead, the potential leaders are identified and then their performance is linked to the enabling and empowerment of others to move up the chain. In other words, the ability to spot talent and identify leaders for the future is done by both the HRM function and the senior management who work in tandem in this effort. Research into these successful companies has shown that the people management in these companies is world class and the contributing factor that differentiates these companies from others is that the HRM function plays a critical role throughout the employee lifecycle and not at the recruitment and training phase alone. The other factor is that the leaders in these companies are expected to have skill sets that match the need for adapting to the challenges of the 21st century business landscape. In other words, these companies groom the leaders of the future right from the middle management level.

Closing Thoughts

Finally, leadership is a combination of natural abilities and the organizational nurturing of the employees with those skills. Hence, this interplay between nature and nurture is what determines the success or otherwise of the HRM function and the senior management efforts to develop leadership in these companies.

Role of HR Manager in People Enabling and People Empowerment

People Enabling and People Empowerment

Until now, we have discussed the role of an HR manager in various processes related to the HR function. The emphasis was on a general overview and a description of the various activities instead of specific details. This discusses a couple of the crucial functions that an HR manager has to perform and those are related to enabling employees to perform to their potential and empowering the employees to lead fulfilling careers. In the earlier decades, organizational theory and practice limited itself to ensuring that employees are well paid and their benefits and other perks taken care of. There was little by way of ensuring personal fulfillment and job satisfaction. This was because of the predominance of manufacturing in the economies of the 1970s and the 1980s which meant that the workforce was to be treated as cogs in the machine instead of assets that the modern day HRM theory and practice follows. With the advent of the services sector, a branch of HRM known as SHRM or Strategic Human Resource Management grew in response to the changing profiles of employees and this approach when combined with the systems approach of management thought meant that the enabling of employees and the empowerment of employees were the buzzwords for HR managers.

Specific Aspects of the Twin Objectives

Concomitant with this trend, the HR managers in most firms these days focus on these aspects by constantly seeking feedback, suggesting improvements, and providing people support to the employees. in multinational companies, it is usually the case that the employees above the team leader level have one-on-ones with the HR staff where all the issues concerning them are discussed threadbare. These meetings also provide the employees with an opportunity to articulate concerns and point to any grievances that they might have with regards to their jobs, work, or the organization in general. The team members are usually assigned a people manager who performs these tasks and ensures that the employees are performing to their potential. Moreover, the HR function in conjunction with the line managers conduct periodic trainings in soft skills like communication, personal relations, and leadership. Indeed, many organizations like Fidelity have established a set protocol for employees to attend leadership development trainings that bring out the leaders in them and groom them as future managers and future CEO's. Hence, the twin objectives of people empowerment and people enabling are thus met in this paradigm.

How this works in the Real World

Of course, this does not mean that the whole situation resembles utopia where employees and the managers along with the HR staff are one big happy family. On the contrary, in most real world settings, the HR managers have a tough time convincing the employees that the organization means well for them and that they ought to look on the bright side of things instead of complaining and being bitter about issues and grievances all the time. This is where the HR managers skills and personality come into the picture as the ability to persuade, enlighten, and if necessary wield the stick play a crucial role in people management. in other words, the HR manager has to tread a fine line between giving in to the employees and following the organizational mandate. This means that a variety of strategies are usually employed by the HR managers that include some of the skills listed above in addition to the personal equations that the HR manager has with the employees.

Closing Thoughts

Finally, people enabling is all about gaining insights into the personalities of the employees and matching them with the organizational requirements. As mentioned earlier, by way of understanding the employees and their motivations and how well these stack up against organizational goals, the HR managers would be able to perform the critical function of people enabling that is very much required in contemporary management practice.

Talent Management by Successful Companies: Insights from Recent Research

Talent Management by Successful Companies

We discussed how successful companies develop and nurture leaders and groom them for higher roles as their career progresses. The role of the HRM function is critical, as there needs to be excellence all around and not just in one area. In other words, it is not enough if a company has a brand image in the market that attracts top quality talent but is not doing well once this talent starts working in the company. Take for instance, the Indian IT behemoth, Infosys. Though working there is a dream come true for many graduates, in recent months, the company has been hit with astounding attrition, as the company is not doing well in terms of retaining and nurturing talent. On the other hand, companies like Microsoft, Google, and Apple not only attract the best talent in the market but also manage them well leading to their practices becoming a model for other companies to follow. **This analyzes the best talent management practices of successful companies and the role of the HRM function in nurturing and grooming talent.**

Some Aspects in Talent Management

The first aspect for global companies is to not be parochial in their hiring practices and instead, welcome diversity by recruiting international talent, employees from different backgrounds, and in general diversify the employee base. Next, is the identification and grooming of high potentials that would give the organization a pool of leaders from which they can draw upon when faced with a situation where leaders are needed. Though this is a practice that is followed in many companies, the successful companies also identify emerging leaders and not only those who have established themselves. The point here is that successful talent management needs the HRM staff and the senior management to draw up a list of potential leaders at both ends of the talent development chain. In other words, these companies start from the lower levels and go on till the middle and senior management levels. The third aspect of successful talent management is the provision of both vertical and horizontal job opportunities for the existing employees. This means that the employees are provided with a menu of career options that would enable them to shift role and find fulfillment in the role of their choice. The reason why this aspect is very important is that often many companies stifle their employees by not providing change of job functions or roles leading to widespread dissatisfaction among the employees.

Creating a Fulfilling Work Culture

The fourth aspect of successful talent management is that these companies provide their employees with a change of work location where the reason for such a move is not to simply move talent to locations where there are shortfalls but also the need for the employee's personal development is taken into consideration. The point here is that successful talent management requires that employees feel privileged working for the company and their needs for self-actualization and fulfillment be taken care of by the company. Indeed, successful companies often have people first policies where the focus is on creating a stimulated and fast-paced environment that encourages and fosters individual growth and the work environment is much more engaging than a workplace that is solely concerned with profits.

Closing Thoughts

Finally, successful companies often have lower attrition rates even if their compensation practices match the industry standard but are not higher than other companies. In other words, as mentioned in the introductory paragraph, successful talent management requires all around excellence in the realms of leadership development, talent management, and performance management. While the first two topics have been covered, the performance management in successful companies would be covered in the next discussion.

Management of Contractors

In recent times, there has been a marked movement towards outsourcing positions within the organization to vendors who would supply resources for the said jobs. These positions and roles are deemed to be those that can be done by resources from outside. And it is here that the contractors step in to do the job that has been outsourced. The phenomenon of using contractors for regular positions is gaining traction by the day and it is common to see many of these temporary workers doing the work that would have otherwise been done by resources employed full time by the organization. The examples of organizations using contractors as a significant portion of their workforce range from the US Defense Department to Microsoft and in India, many IT organizations like IBM employ contractors to get the job done.

Historical Precedent for Temps

Till recently, the practice of hiring contractors or "temps" was restricted to the Administrative and Support functions like HR and Infrastructure management. However, it now encompasses the areas of regular work like project delivery and execution.

The reasons for using contractors range from less overheads to filling a temporary demand that does not need hiring permanent employees. The organization need not provide health benefits and pension benefits to the contractors and hence these costs can be saved. Further, on completion of the project, the contractors can be reverted to their parent organization or the vendor. This means that the hiring organization is not burdened with excess staff.

Issues with Hiring Contractors

There are several issues that pertain to hiring and management of contractors. Many IT companies hold significant "bench" strength as a means of having a buffer when new projects come their way. However, for many mid-sized and small-sized organizations, maintaining bench strength is often a luxury. So, if they anticipate new projects being entrusted to them, they immediately ask the vendor to supply them with the resources that are needed for the new projects. Of course, in reality, there is often a lag between the request for new resources and the resources actually coming on board because of the time taken to screen the contractors and time taken to bring them up to speed regarding the work that needs to be done.

Managing the Vendors

Some issues that need to be considered before going in for contractors pertain to the way in which the liability arising out of non-performance of the contractors is handled, the extent of control that the managers have over vendors and the payment terms and conditions that organizations have with the vendors. It has been found in studies and surveys that contractors and vendors operate in the "grey" areas of the employer-employee relationship and hence managers need to be on their guard when dealing with vendors. Liabilities and punitive actions aimed at vendors usually end up being unresolved because of the way in which the contracts are worded. Hence, it becomes imperative for the organizations to do their "due diligence" before hiring vendors.

To conclude, the practice of hiring vendors is expected to increase and hence there is a need for both sides to sit down and discuss the modalities of the contractual relationship before committing themselves to the same. In this way, disputes over responsibility and accountability can be amicably resolved if the contracts are worded in such a way that there is little room for ambiguity.

Performance Management as a HR Management concept

The very mention of appraisals, reviews and ratings is enough to make seasoned professionals cringe and rejoice alike. For some, these are occasions when they would come out smiling out of the review whereas for others, there is nothing memorable about the whole process. So, what is it that is so important about performance management? For starters, **performance management is the process of reviewing an employee's performance during the preceding year or cycle and deciding where he or she stands as far as their peers in the same band are concerned.** The process of reviewing results, arriving at a rating and then deciding upon the bonus or salary hike is what performance management is all about. Before we look at the topic sentence, it is important to understand what goes into the decision making process and who is involved in the same. Typically, the process of performance management starts a month or two before the appraisal cycle ends. The appraisal cycle can be half-yearly or yearly depending upon the policies of the organization. Further, the appraisal cycle can be based on the calendar year or the financial year i.e. it can run from April to March of the following year or January to December of the same year. In the same vein, it can be half-yearly as well.

There are different **rounds to the appraisal process**.

1. In the first round, the people who participate in an employee's appraisal are the employee and his or her manager. In this round, the manager gives a frank assessment of the employee's performance after giving a chance to the employee to self-assess.

2. The second round consists of the manager and the manager's manager. This round is mostly about deciding the band in which the employee falls post the rating and in comparison with his or her peers. This process of rationalizing the employee's performance with others is called **"normalization"**. In some organizations, this takes place in the third round where the HR manager is involved as well. In any case, the ratings cannot be decided without the HR manager's assent to the same. Once these rounds are over, the bonus level or the salary hike are decided.

What we have described in the above paragraphs is the way the system "ought" to work. However, as any HR professional or Industry magazines would tell you, the performance management process as it exists in many organizations leaves a lot to be desired. In fact, surveys and studies have found that the majority of employee's who quit organizations do so because of differences over their ratings.

In other words, attrition is in many cases a direct consequence of the way in which the performance management process is managed.

The question as to why this happens can be best understood if we understand the dynamics inherent in the process. For instance, despite exhortations from HR professionals and experts about letting personal biases and prejudices affect the process, in many cases, if the manager and the employee do not see eye to eye on many issues, the appraisal and the ratings are the place where this difference of opinion comes out into the open. Further, the organizations are themselves to blame in some cases as the process of "normalization" means a "winner takes all" approach which leaves the moderate performers bracketed with the poor performers. The point here is not to belittle the competitive environment that is the reason for this. On the other contrary, what is needed is a more holistic approach towards performance management that takes into account the varying needs of employee's and a broader appreciation of differing working styles and motivations.

Hiring Strategies followed by Organizations

People are the lifeblood of any organization. Whether the organization is in the traditional sectors like manufacturing or it is a "new economy" based one like IT and ITES, it needs to be staffed with people of caliber and mettle. Hence, the kind of people that an organization hires is critical to the success of the organization. In this respect, **the hiring strategies followed by organizations take on prominence in the competitive business environment of the 21st century.**

Hiring can take place in many ways and at many levels. It can be for entry level positions or "lateral" hiring where people with experience are taken on board. Further, hiring people can be based on competitive exams (entry level) and the personal approach favored by HR managers for senior level positions. In recent times, hiring for the entry level has taken on an entirely new dimension with the campus recruitment procedures that rely on getting the best talent available from the campuses for companies wishing to hire for entry level positions. The other way of hiring is through selective approach where the Staffing department entrusts the placement consultants with the task of identifying potential employees by picking "profiles" from employee databases and the consultants own database as well.

As outlined above, the different hiring strategies are for different levels in the organization. The most niche hiring takes place at senior levels where the essence is discreetness and hence dedicated consultants or HR professionals approach people at higher levels on a one-one basis.

Whatever be the hiring strategy deployed, the essential components of the process remain more or less the same. These include choosing from the available candidates, taking a decision as to the pay and perks, making an offer and finally, getting them "on board". The hiring process ranges from as less a month or so to drawn out affairs for niche placement. The strategic imperatives that underpin hiring depend on the ability of the organization to effectively leverage its reputation, flexibility in the roles that are available, availability of skilled resources and finally, the package that the organization is willing to offer.

Most debates in organizations on the hiring process hinge on the length of time it takes to hire a person for a particular role and the package that the organization is willing to offer. The term "fitment" is often used as HR jargon which is all about whether a particular person is suitable for the role that is being filled and how well he or she "fits" the job profile. One of the reasons for attrition in organizations is the fact that many employees join them with a set of assumptions about their role only to have their hopes dashed in reality. Hence, in recent times, industry experts have focused on this aspect of ensuring that people are hired only if they are of the right fit.

In conclusion, **hiring people is a key component of a company's internal strategy** and hence something that needs detailed attention and focus. We have touched upon the hiring strategies and the overview of the process. In subsequent discussion, we would explore the topic further.

Using Social Media Profiles of Job Applicants for Hiring Decisions

he Advantages of using Information about Job Applicants from Facebook Profiles

In recent years, there has been a noticeable trend among HR professionals to check the information supplied by a job applicant by comparing it with the information available on his or her Social Networking Websites or SNWs profile. While this trend first become apparent in the West and in the United States in particular, it is catching on in the rest of the world as well where recruiters turn to the SNWs profiles of job applicants to verify and seek information about the candidates. Indeed, this trend is both welcome and worrisome as there are potential legal and ethical implications not to mention privacy and security issues. The trend is welcome because the recruiters have a need to know all the information about job applicants' background and suitability especially for sensitive jobs where the job applicant needs to be totally "clean". Further, the trend is welcome because employers can escape the negligent hiring charges that of late have become common in the US. This means that the recruiters can glean information from the SNWs profiles of the job applicants and if there are any serious character or integrity issues, they can spot them right away.

The Disadvantages of using Information about Job Applicants from Facebook profiles

However, the trend of using the Social Networking Websites (SNWs) profiles of job applicants is worrisome, as the recruiters do not have the legal basis of using such profiles without the consent of the job applicants. Further, the recruiters run the risk of being unethical in their approach as well as "lazy" in their recruiting process if they take the information from the SNWs profiles of the job applicants. Apart from this, the job applicants can be discriminated on the basis of gender, race, sexual orientation, and other characteristics. Moreover, the privacy and the sanctity of information that job applicants post on their Facebook and SNWs profiles is compromised. There is also the risk of security as once the recruiters get access to the profiles, information can be hacked by third parties and leaked which means that there are many implications to this practice. Therefore, it is in the interest of all parties if there are proper safeguards that are drawn up to protect both the parties and this process is followed diligently. This means that the recruiters cannot access the SNWs profiles of the candidates without their consent and the job applicants are aware of their rights and disadvantages of posting personal details on their profiles.

What Recruiters can do and how Job Applicants need to Wary

We have discussed the advantages and disadvantages of recruiters accessing the SNWs profiles of the job applicants. Taking the discussion further, **it is advisable for job applicants to be aware of the fact that in the present information age, any details about themselves and their**

friends can be accessed by anyone and hence, they must be careful about the kind of information that they put out on the big bad World Wide Web. Further, for many positions in the US, job applicants are required to undergo a narcotics test, which means that they would be medically tested for traces of any narcotic substances in their bodies. Therefore, a strong world of caution to the job applicants is that they better not reveal what they did last summer especially when they are applying for highly competitive jobs. For recruiters, the word of advice is that they rely on the traditional route of background checks by independent agencies and not only on the SNWs profiles of the job applicants to base their hiring decisions. Finally, whether the information is private or whether it has been obtained illegally and unethically, the fact that such information exists in the internet domain is cause enough for concern.

The Importance of Background Checks while Hiring New Employees

What are Background Checks?

In recent years, corporates have been conducting background checks on potential recruits. Before we launch into a discussion about the importance of these background checks, we will first explain what is meant by background check. To put it simply, **the process of verifying the credentials of new and potential recruits before they are hired constitutes the process of background checks**. Further, background checks are also used to not only to verify whether a particular employee has indeed graduated from a particular college or worked in a particular company, but also to refer to the references that the employee has provided to get an idea about his or her trustworthiness and personality. In other words, background checks are used to determine the integrity and employability of a particular employee by verifying the credentials supplied by him or her and checking them against the actual records. This practice has become common all over the world as many candidates are found to have been fudging their credentials leading to their detection later on during the career and resulting in embarrassment and inconvenience to the companies. It can also lead to scandals when employees have been found to faked their education and experience details.

Background Checks around the World

Apart from this, **background checks were also the norm in the United States and in Europe where centralized databases exist that store the records of all registered employees of the workforce**. For instance, the social security number is used to identify an employee in the database that has all details of his or her education, experience, credit history, details of any brush with law enforcement, and any other pertinent or relevant details. This has helped the companies in the US and in Europe to detect fake profiles of employees and to understand whether potential recruits have been truthful in their declarations before the companies. On the other hand, in Asia (especially in China and India), these background checks were hitherto restricted only in special cases where the companies on suspicion of a particular employee wanted to find out about him or her. However, in recent years, many multinationals have found it prudent to run background checks on all potential recruits as the incidence of employees faking their credentials has become common. Apart from this, the fact that many employees in these countries often change jobs means that there is a need to know the reason for these shifts as the possibility of dubious exits is very real.

The process of Background Checks

The next aspect about running background checks is that corporates usually outsource this process to dedicated service providers that have access to the databases and work force to handle requests for background checks. Of course, many multinationals like Fidelity do this process in house, as the number of employees on their rolls is manageable as far as running background checks is concerned. Many domestic companies still perform cursory checks because they do not have the resources or the time to conduct extensive background checks. This is the reason why large Chinese and Indian companies often have many employees on their rolls that are not what they claim they are. Without getting into the ethical debate, our suggestion is that all companies should conduct background checks as otherwise they would be having a problem on their hands when the past of the employees becomes public in cases of employees with dubious histories.

Concluding Thoughts

For all those students and potential corporate employees, here is a piece of advice. Be careful when you are posting all kinds of stuff on social media as the process of the background checks often involve parsing through the web and online information provided by the potential recruits. Therefore, the next time you want to rave about that rave party where you had a gala time, be careful about what you post online as that can be found during the background check. Finally, remember to be ethical and straightforward about what you declare on your resumes and application forms as otherwise you might get into trouble with your dream companies.

Retention Strategies - Definition and its Components

Any employee retention strategy would necessarily include a plan for redressing employee grievances and ways and means to address employee issues. This would mean that the employees would be enabled to take their issues regarding pay, their work, their role etc. to the HR manager for each division and expect to get a fair hearing in the process. There should be a plan where the HR manager in conjunction with the manager of the employee who has raised the issue works towards resolving the issue.

Components of a Retention Strategy

Taking each of these strategies in turn, job rotation is the practice of moving the employees around divisions and within divisions with a clear emphasis on making sure that they operate in domains other than the ones assigned to them initially. This would mean that the employees get trained on competencies beyond that of their assigned plant and this would lead to greater motivation to pick up additional skills and motivate them to perform better. The importance of grievance redressal and mitigation cannot be emphasised more. This is the most critical and crucial component of the HRM plan as research has shown that an employee with pending issues awaiting resolution is twice more likely to quit the company than the other employees. Hence, all efforts must be made to redress the grievances of the employees.

Grievance Redressal

An effective retention strategy would focus on preventing as well as addressing grievances. Though it is not the contention that all grievances can be prevented, they can be "pre-empted" by actively listening to the employees from time to time. This strategy of "listening" to the employees would revolve around a concept of "one-one" meetings between the employees and the manager and employees and the HR representative for the unit or division. The idea of the regular "one-one" meetings would be to identify potential causes of friction among the employees and any issues they may have vis-à-vis their job and benefits. These issues need to be brought out into the open before they become contentious resulting in the employee feeling frustrated and quitting the job. Hence, all efforts must be made to identify sources of employee dissatisfaction and "hygiene factors" that must be taken care of for proper functioning of the employees.

Ways to Mitigate Job Dissatisfaction

Management theorists often emphasise the fact that one of the **reasons for low employee morale in organizations is the fact that the employees and often feel alienated and cut off from the larger purpose.** The contention is that the employees feel themselves to be part of an impersonal setup and perceive themselves to be unable to make a difference to the whole unit. Hence, there is a need to involve the employees in the larger picture and provide them with perspective on the bigger picture. In engineering units with assembly line manufacturing, the engineer is often responsible for his or her part of the chain and is not in a position to relate to the bigger picture. Hence, there should be effective strategies like job rotation, interaction with other units, timely promotions and cross functional teams wherein the engineers would feel themselves to be contributing to the larger goal of the company.

Strategic Human Resource Management - A Tool to Achieve Organizational Goals

Strategic Human Resource Management is the practice of aligning business strategy with that of HR practices to achieve the strategic goals of the organization. The aim of SHRM (Strategic Human Resource Management) is to ensure that HR strategy is not a means but an end in itself as far as business objectives are concerned. The idea behind SHRM is that companies must "fit" their HR strategy within the framework of overall Business objectives and hence ensure that there is alignment between the HR practices and the strategic objectives of the organization.

Evolution of SHRM

With the advent of new economy industries like IT and the mushrooming of the service sector, organizations all over the world realized that human resources must be viewed as a source of competitive advantage as opposed to treating it much the same way in access to technology or capital is concerned. What this means is that the practice of HRM is being viewed as something that promotes the business objectives of the firms and not merely another factor in the way the firm is managed.

How does SHRM fit in with Strategy?

With the advent of today's economy where services account for a major share of the GDP and the fact that the service sector is essentially people centric, it is imperative that the people first approach be embraced by the organizations for sustainable business strategy. The practice of SHRM demands a proactive and hands on approach by the management as well as the HR department with regards to the entire gamut of activities ranging from staffing and training and development to mentoring and pay and performance management.

The Way SHRM works

If we take real world examples, many organizations in recent times have dedicated "people managers" whose sole function is to look after the enabling and fulfilling needs of the resources. This is a marked change from treating people as just resources to treating people as assets. For instance, Infosys states that people are its assets and the famous statement by Mr. Narayana Murthy, one of the founders of the company that the capital of Infosys walks in every morning and walks out every evening has to be taken in this context.

Elaborating on this point, one finds that organizations tend to leverage upon the capabilities of the people employed there and ensuring that the "human capital" is nourished and nurtured as a source of competitive advantage. This translates into a dedicated HR department and people managers in every group dealing exclusively with employee issues as opposed to treating this as a line management function.

Conclusion

The times when management could arbitrarily dictate terms to the employees and tread upon their rights is something that is not relevant anymore. With the ballooning of the white collar workforce, it becomes necessary for organizations to pay more attention to the needs of the employees more than ever. Finally, the fact that organizations derive their strategy from employees instead of imposing strategy upon them is the essence of SHRM.

Global Human Resource Management - Meaning and Objectives

With the advent of globalization, organizations - big or small have ceased to be local, they have become global! This has increased the workforce diversity and cultural sensitivities have emerged like never before. All this led to the development of Global Human Resource Management.

Even those organizations who consider themselves immune to transactions across geographical boundaries are connected to the wider network globally. They are in one way or the other dependent upon organizations that may even not have heard about. There is interdependence between organizations in various areas and functions.

The preliminary function of global Human Resource Management is that the organization carries a local appeal in the host country despite maintaining an international feel. To exemplify, any multinational / international company would not like to be called as local, however the same wants a domestic touch in the host country and there lies the challenge.

We may therefore, enumerate the **objectives of global HRM as follows:**

1. Create a local appeal without compromising upon the global identity.
2. Generating awareness of cross cultural sensitivities among managers globally and hiring of staff across geographic boundaries.
3. Training upon cultures and sensitivities of the host country.

The **strategic role of Human resources Management** in such a scenario is to ensure that HRM policies are in tandem with and in support of the firm's strategy, structure and controls. Specifically, when we talk of structures and controls the following become worth mentioning in the context of Global HRM.

- **Decision Making:** There is a certain degree of centralization of operating decision making. Compare this to the International strategy, the core competencies are centralized and the rest are decentralized.
- **Co-ordination:** A high degree of coordination is required in wake of the cross cultural sensitivities. There is in addition also a high need for cultural control.
- **Integrating Mechanisms:** Many integrating mechanisms operate simultaneously.

Global HRM and the Staffing Policy

Here also the role is no different i.e. hiring individuals with requisite skills to do a particular job. The challenge here is developing tools to promote a corporate culture that is almost the same everywhere except that the local sensitivities are taken care of.

Also, the deciding upon the top management or key positions gets very tricky. Whether to choose a local from the host country for a key position or deploy one from the headquarters assumes importance; and finally whether or not to have a uniform hiring policy globally remains a big challenge.

Nevertheless an organization can choose to hire according to any of the staffing policies mentioned below:

- **Ethnocentric:** Here the Key management positions are filled by the parent country individuals.
- **Polycentric:** In polycentric staffing policy the host country nationals manage subsidiaries whereas the headquarter positions are held by the parent company nationals.
- **Geocentric:** In this staffing policy the best and the most competent individuals hold key positions irrespective of the nationalities.

Geocentric staffing policy it seems is the best when it comes to Global HRM. The human resources are deployed productively and it also helps build a strong cultural and informal management network. The flip side is that human resources become a bit expensive when hired on a geocentric basis. Besides the national immigration policies may limit implementation.

Global HRM therefore is a very challenging front in HRM. If one is able to strike the right chord in designing structures and controls, the job is half done. Subsidiaries are held together by global HRM, different subsidiaries can function operate coherently only when it is enabled by efficient structures and controls.

Difference between Personnel Management & HRM

Many students of management and laypeople often hear the term HRM or Human Resource Management and wonder about the difference between HRM and the traditional term

Personnel Management. In earlier times, the Personnel Manager of a factory or firm was the person in charge of ensuring employee welfare and interceding between the management and the employees. In recent times, the term has been replaced with HR manager. This looks at the differences in usage and scope of functions as well as the underlying theory behind these nomenclatures. In the section on introducing HRM, we briefly looked at the main differences. We shall look into them in more detail here.

Personnel Management

Traditionally the term personnel management was used to refer to the set of activities concerning the workforce which included staffing, payroll, contractual obligations and other administrative tasks. In this respect, personnel management encompasses the range of activities that are to do with managing the workforce rather than resources. Personnel Management is more administrative in nature and the Personnel Manager's main job is to ensure that the needs of the workforce as they pertain to their immediate concerns are taken care of. Further, personnel managers typically played the role of mediators between the management and the employees and hence there was always the feeling that personnel management was not in tune with the objectives of the management.

Human Resource Management

With the advent of resource centric organizations in recent decades, it has become imperative to put "people first" as well as secure management objectives of maximizing the ROI (Return on Investment) on the resources. This has led to the development of the modern HRM function which is primarily concerned with ensuring the fulfillment of management objectives and at the same time ensuring that the needs of the resources are taken care of. In this way, HRM differs from personnel management not only in its broader scope but also in the way in which its mission is defined. HRM goes beyond the administrative tasks of personnel management and encompasses a broad vision of how management would like the resources to contribute to the success of the organization.

Personnel Management and HRM: A Paradigm Shift ?

Cynics might point to the fact that whatever term we use, it is finally "about managing people". The answer to this would be that the way in which people are managed says a lot about the approach that the firm is taking. For instance, traditional manufacturing units had personnel managers whereas the services firms have HR managers. While it is tempting to view Personnel Management as archaic and HRM as modern, we have to recognize the fact that each serves or served the purpose for which they were instituted. Personnel Management was effective in the "smokestack" era and HRM is effective in the 21st century and this definitely reflects a paradigm shift in the practice of managing people.

Conclusion

It is clear from the above paragraphs that HRM denotes a shift in focus and strategy and is in tune with the needs of the modern organization. HRM concentrates on the planning, monitoring and control aspects of resources whereas Personnel Management was largely about mediating between the management and employees. Many experts view Personnel Management as being workforce centered whereas HRM is resource centered. In conclusion, the differences between these two terms have to be viewed through the prism of people management through the times and in context of the industry that is being studied.

Managing Employee Performance

Introduction

Managing employee performance is one of the key drivers for organizational success in the present context of firms trying to adopt a resource centered view of the organizational. We have seen elsewhere that integrating HRM practices with those of organizational goals and strategy increases the competitive advantages for the firm. Similarly, managing employee performance within the larger framework of organizational goals is critical for organizations that count people among their key assets. As we have been mentioning throughout, firms in the service sector that lay a lot of emphasis on people need to ensure that employee performance is managed in a holistic manner.

A Two Way Street

When we talk about employee performance, we need to remember that it is a two way process that tie in the manager and the employee with the HR manager playing the role of a mediator. For instance, any discussion about employee performance has to include the manager and the employee or the manager and the managed.

Hence, it is imperative that both parties to this transaction realize their responsibilities and work together to ensure that the process is smoothened. In the succeeding sections, we discuss the role of the manager and the employee and how organizational focus on managing employee performance can play a role as well.

The Role of the Manager

The manager has a duty to ensure that his or her management of the employees is free of biases and prejudices. It's been the case across industries and verticals where the employees feel discriminated against leading to attrition, lower employee morale and in the extreme cases, lawsuits against the company. Hence, the manager has to "walk the talk" and not simply pay lip service to the company's policies on employee performance. During the course of working together as a team, there are bound to be instances where friction between the manager and the team and within the team manifests itself. It is incumbent upon the manager to ensure that this does not morph into a corrosive effect that threatens the very existence of the team.

The Role of the Employee

The above section looked at the role of the manager. The manager has a duty to manage the team effectively and so does the employee have corresponding responsibilities as well. Absenteeism, Shirking Work, A negative attitude and a blasé approach to work are some things that the employee must avoid. It is helpful to the employee to know that once he or she is categorized as having an attitude problem, then it would be difficult for the employee to break the perception and perform effectively. This does not mean that the employee has to take whatever comes his or her way. The point here is that the employee must use the channels available for redressal instead of sulking at work if he or she has grievances about the manager.

Organizational Focus

Though the role of the HR manager and the organization seems to be relatively small, it is a fact that organizational goals and culture play a very important part in ensuring that employee performance is managed to the benefit of the organization. Most of us have read about or heard the benefits of working for MNC's (Multinational Companies) in India. The reason why they are highly talked about is the perception among potential and aspiring employees that these companies treat their people well. Though the point here is not to belittle Indian companies, the objective of this section is to highlight the ways in which organizations can shape the treatment of people in theory and practice.

Conclusion

We have seen the centrality of managing employee performance to the success of the organization. If organizations want to cut down on attrition and boost sagging employee morale, the first thing they can do is to ensure that the employee performance management system is streamlined. Only by a focused approach towards this key driver of organizational effectiveness can the firms ensure that they do not lose out on the "war for talent" as well as "retention" of achievers.

Performance Appraisal Process

For many employees working in the organized sector, the term appraisal process conjures images of hope and fear simultaneously. Hope for a better grade and fear about potential downgrading or a bad rating. The weeks leading up to the appraisal are filled with hectic activity when the employees get down to evaluating themselves and prepare to market their achievements during the time for which the appraisal is being conducted. Before launching into the details of the appraisal process and the theory and practice of the same, it is pertinent to understand what the term appraisal process refers to and why it is important for the firm as well as the employees.

What constitutes the Performance Appraisal process ?

The performance appraisal process, simply put, is the time of the year when the employees are evaluated on their performance during the last six months or one year depending upon the timeframe that is set for the same. The performance appraisal process is conducted between the employee and his or her manager for the first round and subsequently between the manager and the manager's manager before going into the third round which involves the above people excluding the

employee but involving the HR manager as well. The various rounds that comprise the appraisal cycle correspond to the different stages of the process culminating in the final grading of the employee.

Appraise and Appraiser

The most important round is the appraisal interview itself (we will discuss more about this in a separate) between the employee and his or her manager. The employee who is being evaluated is called the appraise and the person (usually the manager) who is doing the evaluation is called the appraiser. The appraiser and appraise prepare themselves for this round by doing a self evaluation (by the appraise) and an objective evaluation (by the appraiser). This is the round in which the most important achievements as well as glaring failures on the part of the appraise are discussed threadbare and usually the employee's role in the process is limited to this round.

What is the outcome of the Appraisal Process ?

As outlined above, the outcome of the appraisal process is the grade that is decided for the employee as well as the salary hike or the bonus potential that is awarded to the employee. Typically, organizations divide the year in which the employee's performance is evaluated into two cycles, one for deciding the salary hike and the other for deciding how much bonus he or she gets for the cycle. In this way, organizations ensure that there is no overlap in grading the employee and a fair and balanced evaluation is the desired outcome though this does not always happen in reality.

Shortcomings of the Appraisal Process

The successful completion of the appraisal process hinges on all the participants approaching the same with an intention to contribute positively instead of bringing personal biases and prejudices to the table. Management experts usually prescribe a set of do's and don'ts to the participants in order to have an harmonious process. However, as has been pointed out above, the process itself is not without its shortcomings and the expecting the participants to be rational and objective at all times is indeed difficult. Further, since most organizations decide the grades in a way similar to the b-school equivalent of Relative Grading instead of absolute ratings, an element of competitive rivalry creeps into the process making some employees unhappy.

For many employees working in the organized sector, the term appraisal process conjures images of hope and fear simultaneously. Hope for a better grade and fear about potential downgrading or a bad rating. The weeks leading up to the appraisal are filled with hectic activity when the employees get down to evaluating themselves and prepare to market their achievements during the time for which the appraisal is being conducted. Before launching into the details of the appraisal process and the theory and practice of the same, it is pertinent to understand what the term appraisal process refers to and why it is important for the firm as well as the employees.

What constitutes the Performance Appraisal process ?

The performance appraisal process, simply put, is the time of the year when the employees are evaluated on their performance during the last six months or one year depending upon the timeframe that is set for the same. The performance appraisal process is conducted between the employee and his or her manager for the first round and subsequently between the manager and the manager's manager before going into the third round which involves the above people

excluding the employee but involving the HR manager as

well. The various rounds that comprise the appraisal cycle correspond to the different stages of the process culminating in the final grading of the employee.

Appraise and Appraiser

The most important round is the appraisal interview itself (we will discuss more about this in a separate) between the employee and his or her manager. The employee who is being evaluated is called the appraise and the person (usually the manager) who is doing the evaluation is called the appraiser. The appraiser and appraise prepare themselves for this round by doing a self evaluation (by the appraise) and an objective evaluation (by the appraiser). This is the round in which the most important achievements as well as glaring failures on the part of the appraise are discussed threadbare and usually the employee's role in the process is limited to this round.

What is the outcome of the Appraisal Process ?

As outlined above, the outcome of the appraisal process is the grade that is decided for the employee as well as the salary hike or the bonus potential that is awarded to the employee. Typically, organizations divide the year in which the employee's performance is evaluated into two cycles, one for deciding the salary hike and the other for deciding how much bonus he or she gets for the cycle. In this way, organizations ensure that there is no overlap in grading the employee and a fair and balanced evaluation is the desired outcome though this does not always happen in reality.

Shortcomings of the Appraisal Process

The successful completion of the appraisal process hinges on all the participants approaching the same with an intention to contribute positively instead of bringing personal biases and prejudices to the table. Management experts usually prescribe a set of do's and don'ts to the participants in order to have an harmonious process. However, as has been pointed out above, the process itself is not without its shortcomings and the expecting the participants to be rational and objective at all times is indeed difficult. Further, since most organizations decide the grades in a way similar to the b-school equivalent of Relative Grading instead of absolute ratings, an element of competitive rivalry creeps into the process making some employees unhappy.

Performance Appraisal Interview

Introduction

We have discussed the performance appraisal process in earlier. we discuss the performance appraisal interview and its importance in the performance appraisal cycle. The performance appraisal interview is the first round in the performance appraisal process and this is the round in which the manager communicates his evaluation of the employee's performance during the appraisal period or the time that the employee's performance is being evaluated.

What is a Performance Appraisal Interview ?

A performance appraisal interview is the first stage of the performance appraisal process and involves the employee and his or her manager sitting face to face to discuss threadbare all aspects of the employee's performance and thrash out any differences in perception or evaluation. The performance appraisal interview provides the employee with a chance to defend himself or herself against poor evaluation by the manager and also gives the manager a chance to explain what he or she thinks about the employee's performance.

In a nutshell, the performance appraisal interview precedes the normalization process and is subsequent to the employee filling up the evaluation form and the manager likewise doing so. The interview is the stage where both sides debate and argue the employees' side of the story as well as the manager's perception.

Objective Evaluation versus Personal Biases

Though management theorists like to propound the benefits of objective evaluation, it is a fact in contemporary organizations that an element of personal bias enters the evaluation. This is evident from the studies and surveys done by HR consultants like Hewitt that point to the employee's dissatisfaction with the performance appraisal process as one of the main reasons for leaving the company. To curb the incidence of biases and heuristics playing a role in the appraisal, HR managers typically conduct orientations and trainings to both the Managers and the Employees to sensitize them to these dangers that are sometimes inherent in the process.

On the other hand, the employees' should approach the process without unrealistic expectations and expect the Manager to agree to whatever they write on the performance evaluation form. Hence, there is a need for both sides in the interview process to approach the same with an open mind and be as objective as possible. However, this is easier said than done and hence organizations expend resources on making the process as transparent and objective as possible.

The Right and Wrong Way to Approach a Performance Appraisal Interview

The performance appraisal interview must be taken seriously and both the employee and the manager must set aside time to go through the process. The manager cannot arbitrarily change the time or the venue and must not approach the interview in a haphazard manner. Despite all these injunctions, it is often the case that the manager has to be reminded about the interview and then he or she hurriedly arranges the meeting. This is definitely the wrong way to approach the interview. Further, the manager must make the time to go through the employees' self evaluation and rate the same objectively.

Though there is no right way to conduct the performance appraisal interview, it is incumbent upon the manager to avoid the pitfalls described above. A rule of thumb would be set aside a few days to conduct all the interviews with members of his or her team and ensure follow-ups to the process. The follow-up is needed when the employee is not satisfied with the interview discussion and hence requests for additional time to debate the rating. In some cases, the HR manager may need to step in to ensure that the process is concluded to the satisfaction of the employee and the manager.

Conclusion

Surveys have shown that nearly 70% of the employees who leave organizations cite the bad rating that they have got as the reason for quitting and often voice their disappointment at the process in the exit interview. Hence, there is a need for organizations to smoothen the performance appraisal process and since the performance appraisal interview is the first step; the beginning must be made well. Since the career progression of employees depends on the ratings that they get, the whole process must be taken seriously by all the stakeholders.

Managing Employee Relations

Literally speaking **employee relations consists of all those areas in Human resource Management that involves**

general relationship with the workforce. This may be in the form of collective or mutual agreements that leads to the formation of trade unions or through policies and procedures for employee engagement and communication.

The increased growth of workforce diversity has led to a need for continuous changes in HR practices and policies. Managing human relations has become the most difficult challenge that the managers are facing today. Conflicts within the organization, small or large have become inevitable. This can be overcome by developing sound interpersonal and conflict management skills within you.

Furthermore employee relations strategies are made in order to overcome these problems. These strategies define the objectives of the organization to manage its relationships with employee and all other organizations. These strategies are aimed at enhancing the overall quality of employee management and ensuring their participation and continuous improvement.

Establishing and maintaining harmonious relationships with employees, managers need to develop skills that focus on interpersonal communication and conflict management. In addition to this, they need to define and establish such policies and procedures that go well with the diversity of workforce. It is evident that maintaining diverse workforce and understand their psychology has been emerged as one of the biggest challenges for managers. The impact of globalization can be seen on every organization and in every part of the world.

In today's times, it is really the toughest business for managers to deal efficiently with employees. Failing to do so can result in high attrition rate. To retain and get the maximum output from them, managers need to improve their skills such as active listening, effective communication, acceptability, adaptability, decision-making and conflict management. These are the core skills that supervisors and managers can use tactfully to resolve conflicts among employees or between employees and organization.

However developing or improving above mentioned skills does not guarantee a smooth and conflict-free working environment because conflict is the hard core truth that can not avoided fully. It is but natural to have conflicts and clashes where different people from different backgrounds and cultures come together and work. Still, we can focus on developing these skills in order to manage employee relations to the extent possible:

- **Interpersonal Skills:** Effective communication is an art as well science to mend spoiled relationships among employees as well as between employee and employer. This is the foundation for all the actions taken by a manager to establish and manage human relations in an organization. Working with diverse workforce, understanding their psychologies, needs and requirements requires tremendous amount of effort as well as interaction. It is the first step to break the ice and move ahead in a positive direction. It helps managers create a peaceful working environment in the organization.

- **Conflict Management:** Learning to manage conflicts can help managers resolve employee relations issues quickly and effectively. Listening patiently both the sides and arriving upon a decision that can satisfy both parties can help greatly. A manager should avoid jumping straight to the conclusion, making hasty decisions and boosting the ego of one party. This can lead to bigger or never ending conflict. Effective communication, efforts to reach to the truth and making right decisions are some of the qualities that a manager needs to possess to resolve the conflicts among employees forever.

Employees are the most important assets of any organization-big or small. Managing employee relations effectively can help organizations achieve their goals faster.

Employee Rewards and Recognition

Ask yourself the importance of a chocolate or a muffin to motivate your child to finish his homework or clean his room. Same way, the rewards and recognition can prove to be extremely beneficial to keep your employees motivated to perform extraordinary, achieve the targets and stick to the organization.

The power of employee recognition can not be underestimated especially when they have thousands of lucrative opportunities in front of them.

Who doesn't want to attract, hire and retain the best talents of the industry? Why not explore the new ways to foster employee motivation and drive them to achieve their targets then? After all an organization's performance is directly related to the performance of its human resources. This is a simple logic; if you make their day, they make your organization.

Employee rewards and recognition system is not just a positive thing to do with people but communicating it effectively is an efficient tool in encouraging them to create and bring business for you. Treating your employees like your assets and maintaining harmonious relationships with them doesn't only yield business in present but also an effective strategy for future. Employers and management need to be pro-active to develop a talented and dedicated workforce that can take you to your goals.

Fulfilling employees' needs, recognizing their efforts and presenting them with monetary and non-monetary rewards help you create a right workforce for your organization that can be your partner in success. Recognition of their efforts and boosting their morale results in increased productivity and decreased attrition rate. It is a proven fact that the motivated and dedicated workforce can change the fate of a company. After all, human effort is the biggest contributing factor in success of any organization. It is just next to impossible to achieve organizational goals only by the efforts of top management. It's the workforce who executes their plans and helps them achieve their financial as well as non-financial aims.

Establishing and implementing a reward system needs careful analysis of the company policies and procedures. Deciding how to recognize employees' efforts and what to provide them requires thorough analysis of responsibilities and risks involved in a particular job. Reward system of an organization should also be in alignment with its goals, mission and vision. Depending upon the job profile, both monetary and non-monetary rewards can encourage employees to contribute more to the organization.

- **Monetary Rewards:** A raise in salary, incentives, movie tickets, vacation trips, monetary allowances on special occasions, redeemable coupons, cash bonuses, gift certificates, stock awards, free or discounted health check-ups for the entire family and school/tuition fees for employees' children fall in this category. While designing company policies for monetary rewards, management should make sure that benefits should be as broad-based as possible. It requires sound planning and effective implementation.

- **Non-monetary Rewards:** Non-monetary rewards may include trophies, certificates, letters of appreciation, dinner with boss, redecoration of employee cabin, membership of recreation clubs, perks, use of company facilities, suggestion awards, tie-pins, brooches, diaries, promotion, say in management, etc.

A combination of monetary and non-monetary rewards can work wonders and drive employees to perform well continuously. A proper and efficient employee reward and recognition program can establish harmonious relationships between employees and employer.

Variable Pay and Performance Linked Incentives

Variable Pay - Then and Now

The practice of linking pay to performance has been around for a while. However, what's new is that the percentage of pay that is linked to performance and the way in which the same is structured around different components of performance is new.

We all know about the system of increments and bonuses in the Government and Public Sector. These were designed in such a way that the employee's performance is rewarded proportionally. However, the quantum of bonus and increments was so small that it hardly had an effect on the pure play linking pay to performance. The resulting inefficiencies in the government and public sector have been extensively reported.

In recent times, the concept of linking pay to performance has taken on an entirely new dimension with the introduction of variable pay. This discusses some aspects of the variable pay and performance linked incentives in place in the contemporary organizations.

How it Works

One of the key components of this variable pay plan is the strategy of linking pay to performance. This is a strategy that has been followed by many Multinational companies across the world and consists of the overall pay structure being broken down into components. These components would include the basic pay, benefits and the variable pay. The variable pay would be paid out as a percentage of the whole subject to the performance of the employee. For instance, if the employee gets a grade of 2 on a scale of 1 to 4, the variable pay would be 70-80% of the eligible amount and if the employee gets a grade of 1, the variable pay would be 120-100% of the eligible amount. Accordingly, the performance of the employee determines the variable component of the salary. The international practice is to increase the component of the variable pay higher according to the hierarchy. This would mean that at senior levels of the employee hierarchy, the variable component can be as high as 50-60% of the overall pay.

Categories of Variable Pay

Further, there can be different categories of variable pay. The first component of the variable pay can be linked to individual performance, the second component can be linked to division performance and the third component can be linked to company performance. The idea behind variable pay is that it provides an incentive for employees to feel a sense of ownership and take responsibility for their jobs as well and relate to the overall division and company. By introducing variable pay, the management would ensure that employees are motivated to contribute individually and as a unit and a division and finally as part of the whole company. As outlined in the section on retention strategy, the sense of alienation of the employees can be reduced by making them feel part of a whole and not treat them as individual "cogs in the machine".

Conclusion

In conclusion, this discussed variable pay and performance linked incentives as a necessary evolution to a system where merit is recognized more than it is being done now. Given the fact that many organizations in India follow this approach, it is time for the employees and prospective employees to attune themselves to this concept and work accordingly.

Why Diversity ?

With the advent of globalization, it has become imperative for organizations to have a workforce that is composed of different ethnicities and with the maturing of the business paradigm; gender is no longer a constraint. This has prompted large scale changes in the way organizations recruit people.

Further, in many countries the laws governing corporates have been legislated in such a way that makes the firms actively encourage diversity. For instance, the US is the leading proponent of diversity with the adoption of the "Equal Opportunity Act". This act mandates employers not to discriminate on any basis be it gender, color, lifestyle preferences or any other traits as mentioned in the act. This has given a fillip to the employment of women and people of color and has removed the barriers that were threatening to make these groups of people at a minority in the corporate world as well.

Still a long way to go

Though the laws mandate equal opportunity, in practice, the hiring of disadvantaged and minority groups is still lagging behind in relative terms when compared with the majority groups. For instance, it is not uncommon for employers to weed out resumes of women and people of color. In India, there are still barriers to the hiring of people from certain states as was evidenced in news reports that emanated in the recent past. These practices are certainly undesirable and cast a cloud about the intentions of employers in embracing diversity at the workplace. Further, given the spate of lawsuits about sexual discrimination and harassment on the basis of ethnicity, it becomes clear that more than laws that deal with these issues, we need a mindset change among the firms and the practice of diversity is something that has to be encouraged from the top.

Some suggestions

Among the ways in which employers can encourage diversity is by promoting the concept of "blind resumes" that do not have the name, gender or ethnicity of the applicant mentioned. This would ensure that recruiters screen the resumes on the basis of the applicants' qualifications alone and other factors are secondary. Another way to ensure diversity is by sensitizing the workforce to gender and ethnic issues, and ensure that they are more tolerant of people who are unlike them.

Conclusion

In conclusion, one needs to understand the difference between having a policy of diversity and actually practicing it by comparing it to the adage about the difference between the letter of the law and the spirit of the law. Only by ensuring that the law is followed in spirit as well can employers truly embrace diversity.

Managing Workforce Diversity

Introduction

We live in times when global corporations and their reach across the world bring benefits in terms of innovative HR policies as well as challenges in terms of managing the workforce are concerned. The rise of such corporations means that the workforce is composed of diverse races and ethnicities. Further, the issue of gender diversity in terms of more women participating in the workforce has been a trend that has accelerated in the last two decades in India and much earlier in the developed countries. This looks at the reasons for managing workforce diversity and the issues that such management brings to the fore.

Why is Management of Diversity Important ?

When an organization has people of different ethnicities and a greater proportion of women than the industry average, naturally the question arises as to how to reconcile the differences between these employees without causing too much friction in everyday interactions. Managing diversity is important as otherwise the performance of the organization takes a hit and worse, there can be possible lawsuits and

Legal tangles from disaffected employees who feel aggrieved because of instances of discrimination and harassment based on their ethnicity or gender.

Issues in Managing Diversity

One of the central issues in managing diversity is to do with the majority and the minority perspective. Usually, it is the case in organizations that there is a predominant majority of a particular race or ethnicity and various others in minority groups. And considering that the most pressing issue in managing diversity arises out of the treatment of women, we get a sense of the issues of race and gender as the primary drivers in managing diversity. In recent times, these issues have come to the forefront of the debate because of greater awareness among the minority groups about their rights as well as stricter enforcement of laws and regulations that govern workplace behavior.

Hence, it is in the interest of the management of any firm to sensitize their workforce towards race and gender issues and ensure that the workplace is free of discrimination against minority groups as well as women.

Gender Sensitization

We have devoted a separate section on gender sensitization because when compared to other issues in managing diversity, this is the most pressing issue because of the preponderance of women in the workforce as well as recent trends that point to the emergence of this single issue as the dominant issue that is taking the mind space of managers. The worrying aspect about this issue is that despite policies and rules governing gender specific issues in most organizations, there is little evidence to show that they are being followed. Hence, what is needed is a mindset change rather than more policies and this can only be done if the workforce is sensitized to the needs of women.

Conclusion

Though the situation in Corporate India or India Inc. has not yet reached the stage where lawsuits are routinely brought against management for discriminatory practices, nonetheless, the trend in recent years is towards a more vocal disapproval of such practices from industry leaders and management consultants who repeatedly emphasize the importance of a non-discriminatory workplace. Hence, the onus is on the management, senior and middle, to ensure that they follow the norms that is required of them. In our opinion, the middle management and the managers who directly interact with the teams of people have a greater role as they are the "Sandwich" between the upper management and the workforce and hence are in a position to follow the policies as well as enforce them.

Workplace Health and Safety

Statistics show that every twenty seconds of every working minute throughout the world, someone dies as a result of industrial accident or poor safety conditions at workplace. Thousands of employees throughout the world lose their limbs, suffer from temporary or permanent disability or lose their lives due to insufficient arrangements for their health and safety at workplace. Not only workers but their families also suffer the loss all through their lives.

December 1984 witnesses the world's worst chemical disaster in Bhopal, India, when a methylisocyanate gas leaked from the Union Carbide plant in the city. It killed over 4,000 people and not hundreds but thousands suffered from permanent health damage. The haunting memories of this disaster are still fresh in our minds.

Not only insufficient arrangements of workers' health and safety at workplace have taken away their lives but these days stress at workplace is also emerging as a major culprit of spoiling employees and their families' lives. Every now and then we hear of suicide cases of individuals from the corporate world. Does mental stress not a factor that should be considered with physical health and safety provisions? Have workers' lives become so cheap that small issues can take away their lives leaving their families wracked, children orphaned and parents shocked with disbelief ?

Does safety at workplace only mean to protect the workers from the danger of accidents or any other mishaps? Should workplace safety not consider mental stress or emotional trauma or personal issues of employees? Is the physical presence of an employee enough for an employer to run the business?

There is no end to these questions. In today's fast-paced life and cut-throat competition, employers need to rethink about safety provisions at workplace. It not only refers to the absence of accidents. Rather, the concept expands to both physical and mental safety of the employees. It is possible to show the external injury but what about something that is suffocating the employees from inside?

Providing safety to the employees at workplace has a moral dimension as well. Though it is a legal requirement and fetches monetary compensation in case of failure but it can't bring back an individual's life. Eliminating the causes of accidents and counseling employees at workplace play a substantial role in saving the operating costs, increasing productivity and ensuring reliability and dependability from the employees.

Employees are the biggest assets of any organization and few well managed and co-coordinated safety programs can minimize the loss and damage to them as well as to the organization. With basic safety policies and remedies for accidents, the companies should also provide systematic training to industrial employees so that they are able to do their jobs efficiently and safely.

Over a few years, even the mental health of employees, particularly at executive level, has grabbed the attention of the employers. Mental breakdowns because of stress, tension and work pressure, depression resulting from failure to meet targets and mental illness taking toll from alcoholism and poor human relations have consumed many brilliant young executives. The need is to provide psychiatric counseling, co-operation and consultation. Development and maintenance of effective human relations can work wonders. Therefore, while making arrangements for physical health and safety at workplace, employers should also take actions to improve mental health of their indispensable resource.

Workplace Safety Programs

Effective designing and implementation of workplace safety programs can minimize the loss and damage caused to persons and property by eliminating the risk of industrial accidents. In addition to it, the employee safety programs can result in substantial cost savings, increased productivity and establishing harmonious relations with workers.

For designing effective safety plans and implementing them requires thorough analysis of workplace conditions and determining the level of protection required. The degree of protection depends upon the degree of risk involved in any job. For example, people working in mines require more safety that those working in a BPO. It also depends on the kind of job the person is engaged in. Sales personnel may require higher level of protection than the one in any administrative job.

Workplace safety programs are not only effective in

eliminating the risk of damage caused to person but is also an effective tool in retaining the existing and attracting new talent from the industry. Who doesn't want a safe and healthy work environment? Around 90 percent of working professionals seek safety at workplace rather than a fat package.

Organizations can reduce the risk of accidents at workplace by identifying the level of risk, modifying the already existing policy and implementing it effectively. For this, it needs to design proper and efficient management programs to improve physical environment employee assistance programs to help them diagnose and treat their stress-related problems.

Here is a mention of few workplace safety programs that are implemented by top-notch organizations to ensure workers' physical and mental safety:

- **Safety Policy:** It contains a declaration of the employer's intent towards the safety of employees and means to realize it. It includes causes, extent and remedies for accidents at workplace. The policy specifies the company's goals and responsibilities and caveats and sanctions for failing to fulfill them.

- **Provision of Physical Health Services:** Many organizations render periodical physical health check-up services to their employees. Regular medical check-ups of employees help detect the signs and symptoms of tension, stress, ulcers, depression and other diseases resulting from the exposure to harmful gases or other irritants.

It is considered as one of the major steps to control occupational health hazards and treat them before they become worse. In addition to this, it helps managers in rehabilitating the employees by redesigning their jobs in order to eliminate the further damage to their health.

- **Mental Health Services:** In order to reduce the risk of mental breakdowns because of tension, pressure and depression and mental illness, a mental health service is provided to the employees in different ways such as psychiatric counseling, co-operation and consultation with specialists, educating employees about the importance of mental health and establishment, development and maintenance of harmonious human relations at workplace.

- **Employee Assistance Programs:** These are specially designed to deal with stress-related problems of the employees and help in diagnosis, treatment, screening and prevention of both work and non-work related problems. These programs provide real help to professionals and do not carry any negative implications.

- **Fitness Programs:** These programs focus on overall health of employees and include both disease identification as well as lifestyle modification. The most common programs carried out by the organizations are hypertension identification, physical fitness, exercise, nutrition, smoking and drinking cessation, diet control and personal and work-related stress management.

- **Awareness Programs:** Conducting the workshops about sexually transmitted diseases such as HIV AIDS help a lot in raising the awareness of employees towards such dreadful diseases. Such programs clear out the confusion and disruption in the workforce.

We all must have heard of a simple phrase, "Health is Wealth." This is true for individuals as well as organizations. Understanding, developing, implementing and evaluating workplace safety programs not only helps individuals in maintaining their health but also helps organizations in retaining their resources.

An Online Guide to OSHA Safety Regulations, Standards and Checklist

Occupational Safety and Health Administration, an agency of the United States Department of Labor, was created on December 30, 1970. Formed under the Occupational Safety and Health Act, its mission is to ensure safe and healthy conditions at workplace in order to prevent work-related illness, injuries, diseases and wrongful deaths by setting and implementing safety standards and by educating people by providing training and assistance.

Who Is Covered Under OSHA Regulations ?

OSH Act covers both employers and employees in most private and public sector workplaces either directly through federal OSHA or through an OSHA approved State Program. These regulations are industry-specific and task-specific to prevent or reduce workplace hazards or accidents resulting in illness, injuries or deaths in severe cases. The guidelines help employers recognize risk factors at workplace and take steps to control them. On the other hand, OSHA guidelines also take care of employees' rights.

The self-employed persons, employees of State and local governments except those who work in one of the states with OSHA-approved safety and health programs, people employed in mining, nuclear energy production and nuclear weapons manufacturing and other segments where working conditions are regulated by Federal Agencies and farms where only family members are employed are not covered by OSH Act.

What Does OSHA Safety Manual Include ?

OSHA publishes a Safety Manual that is developed by an experienced team of doctors, attorneys and safety consultants. The manual includes detailed information about OSHA, its policies and procedures, OSHA standards, regulations as well as legislation. In addition to this, it also contains guidelines about Health & Safety Procedures, Industries Covered under

OSHA, Basic Provisions and Requirements, Federal OSHA standards, Risk Assessment Forms and Instructions, Health and Safety Policies, Employee and Employer Rights and Responsibilities, Codes of Practice, Workplace Inspection, Penalties, Hazard Tables, Appeals Process and Relation to State, local and other Federal laws.

What Is OSHA Checklist ?

OSHA Safety Inspection Checklist is designed specially for the employers to help them meet OSHA safety requirements at workplace. It covers various regulations that apply to almost all businesses such as sanitation requirements, aisle way requirements, exit route signs, information about nearby toxic substances and radiations, fire alarm systems with fire sprinkler systems and their maintenance, maintenance of workplace injuries and work-related illness records, pasting safety posters with emergency contact numbers and regular inspection of power tools, equipments, air compressors and lighting system.

The employers covered under OSHA directly or indirectly need to look over their workplaces and meet OSHA safety requirements to avoid any legal action against them. They should carefully go through the OSHA Safety Inspection Checklist, arrange for required provisions and get a safety inspection done.

OSHA Training And Education

Every year OSHA identifies the areas where OSHA standards for safety and health in workplace are not met. The organization sends them notice to conduct training and educational programs for workers. It also invites grant applications form non-profit groups and other organizations to address these needs. It provides funds to them so that they can reach out to their employees and conduct workplace training and educational programs. OSHA also offers consultation assistance to employers for establishing and maintaining a safe workplace.

HR Challenges - How to cope with them efficiently ?

Human Resource Management used to be considered as other conventional administrative jobs. But over a period of time, it has evolved as a strategic function to improve working environment, plan out human resources needs and strike a balance between the organization and employers in order to increase organizational productivity and meet organizational goals. Not to exaggerate but in today's highly competitive world it has gradually become one of the most important functions of an organization.

It is really a huge challenge to understand the psychology of workforce, retain the best talents of the industry, motivate them to perform better and handle diversity while maintaining unity simultaneously, especially in countries like India, where it is still evolving. Globalization has resulted in many positive developments but it has left many concerns for HR managers.

In today's tough world and tight job market, coordinating a multicultural or diverse workforce is a real challenge for HR department.

Human resource managers are on their toes to strike a balance between employer and employees keeping in mind the recent trends in the market. They may find themselves in dire consequences if they are not able to handle the human resource challenges efficiently.

To remain in business, **human resource managers need to efficiently address following human resource challenges:**

- **Handling Multicultural / Diverse Workforce:** Dealing with people from different age, gender, race, ethnicity, educational background, location, income, parental status, religious beliefs, marital status and ancestry and work experience can be a challenging task for HR managers. With this, managing people with different set of ideologies, views, lifestyles and psychology can be very risky. Effective communication, adaptability, agility and positive attitude of HR managers can bind the diverse workforce and retain talents in the organization.

- **Managing Change:** Who wants to change their ideology or way of working? Neither you nor I. How can we expect others to change then? Bringing change in organizational processes and procedures, implementing it and then managing it is one of the biggest concerns of HR managers. Business environment is so volatile. Technology keeps changing every now and then. All thanks to globalization. Upgrading the existing technology and training people for them is a real headache for HR department. The success rate of technology change depends how well HRD can handle the change and manage people issues in the process.

- **Retaining the Talents:** Globalization has given freedom to working professionals to work anywhere in the world. Now that they have endless lucrative opportunities to work, hiring and retaining the best industry talent is no joke. Maintaining harmonious relations with them, providing excellent work environment and offering more remuneration and perks than your competitors can retain and motivate them.

- **Conflict Management:** HR managers should know how to handle employee-employer and employee-employee conflicts without hurting their feelings. Although it is almost impossible to avoid conflicts among people still handling them tactfully can help HR managers to resolve the issues. They should be able to listen to each party, decide and communicate to them in a convincing manner in order to avoid future conflicts.

HR professional must be proactive with all strategies and action plans in order to meet the changing needs of the organization. They must be thorough with the basic functions of HR including planning, organizing, leading and controlling human resources.

Human Resource Audit - Meaning, Phases and its Advantages

Human Resource Audit is a comprehensive method of objective and systematic verification of current practices, documentation, policies and procedures prevalent in the HR system of the organization. An effective HR audit helps in identifying the need for improvement and enhancement of the HR function. It also guides the organization in maintaining compliance with ever-changing rules and regulations. HR audit, thus, helps in analyzing the gap between 'what is the current HR function' and 'what should be/could be the best possible HR function' in the organization.

Though HR auditing is not mandatory like financial auditing, yet, organizations these days are opting for regular HR audits in order to examine the existing HR system in line with the organizations policies, strategies and objectives, and legal requirements. HR auditor can be internal or external to the organization. Generally, HR consulting firms render the service of external HR auditors.

It is necessary for the top management to establish the terms and scope of the audit clearly before the external firm to make the audit successful. This includes defining the exact purpose of audit, viz. examining compliance with legal requirements and organization's policies, identifying problem areas to avoid crisis situation with appropriate planning, analyzing ways to better serve the needs of relevant parties – employees, partners or society, measuring the work processes, seeking HR related opportunities available within the organization, dealing with situation of merger and acquisitions, etc.

Primary components of the HR system which are generally audited include – documentation, job descriptions, personnel policies, legal policies, recruitment and selection, training and development, compensation and employee benefit system, career management, employee relations, performance measurement and evaluation process, termination, key performance indicators, and HR Information Systems (HRIS).

The entire process of HR auditing is broadly segmented in following phases, pre-audit information, on-site review, records review, and audit report.

The first three phases involve extensive collection of quantitative as well as qualitative information. The method for collection of information depends upon the size of the target audience, availability of time and type of data to be collected.

The pre-audit information phase includes a review of the organization's policies, HR manuals, employee handbooks, reports, etc. which form the basis of working in the organization. The next phase of on-site review, involves questionnaires, interviews, observation, informal discussions, surveys, or a combination of such methods to get the necessary inputs from the members of the organization. The records review phase requires detailed scanning of current HR records, employees' files, employee absenteeism and turnover statistics, notices, compensation claims, performance assessments, etc.

Utilizing the data so collected, the HR checklist is completed which is the widely used method for carrying out HR audit. In the checklist method, a list of all the system particulars under audit, viz. the policies, procedures, or practices, is created in a sequential manner. Against each particular item, the actual practice as followed by the organization is mentioned. The defined practice and the actual practice are then compared to determine compliance between the two as well as analyzing the deviation from compliance. On the basis of this analysis, the final audit report is complied with appropriate conclusions and recommendations highlighting the strengths and weaknesses of the HR function along with the necessary improvements as required.

HR audit, thus, contributes towards the best possible use of internal resources and maximizing the effectiveness of human capital in the organization. At the same time, it is useful in streamlining the HR processes and practices with the industry best practices and standards.

HRM: Hiring in the Shadow of Stagnating Growth

How the times have changed for potential recruits

There was a time in the late 1990s and early 2000s when the software companies were hiring anyone with some basic computer skills. A popular joke that did the rounds was about a leading software company having the message of "Trespassers would be recruited". Such was the demand for software professionals that graduate from all fields were eager to join the bandwagon. The situation now is completely different with stringent entry norms, raising the skills bar, and paying the minimum salaries instead of large pay packets and associated benefits.

Indeed, **there is a sea change from the time when candidates used to take calls from other companies when the interview for a particular company was going on**. This is an indication of the change from the exuberant times in the 1990s and the early 2000s to the present where the overall mood is of stagnation and low growth.

Hiring Strategies in a Low Growth Economy

The hiring strategies have similarly changed with the change in the economic scenario. Earlier, the HR function used to be given a target of the number of employees to be recruited in a specified period and their performance and the bonuses were measured in terms of how well they met these targets. The present scenario is one where the HR function is given qualitative limits instead of quantitative limits. What this means is that quality matters more than numbers and companies are no longer tolerating low skilled or low quality candidates. This has increased the pressure on both the recruiters as well as the HR functions. Whereas in earlier years, the pressure was on finding the high number of people required, now the pressure is on finding the right candidate.

Some Strategies for fresh graduates

These trends have implications for those who are graduating now and those who have graduated in the last couple of years. The best bet even now remains campus interviews and targeted placements as these avenues of recruitment are still numbers driven. The other aspect is that the fresh graduates have to invest their time and effort in upgrading their skills and learning more skills as that would make them stand out from the competition. The key aspect here is that one must be distinctive in order to score over the competition and as the hiring now is tougher and based on finding the fit between the employee and the role, it is advisable to study the requirements of the role thoroughly and then prepare for the test and the interview accordingly.

Closing Thoughts

Finally, when times are tough, the tough get going and so, the hiring of those with mental toughness and the ability to work under pressure is the norm. Apart from this, the fact that the hiring is more location based because of various factors means that proximity to the major cities would be an added advantage. The recent encouragement of the development of Tier Two cities means that candidates who are not near to the cities can still benefit if they are located in these up and coming cities.

The Challenges of Managing Attrition in Contemporary Organizations

The Reasons for Attrition

In recent months, there has been a spate of news items about how attrition is taking its toll on many organizations in Asia and especially in the IT sector in India. Whereas in the west, because of the recession and the gloomy economic conditions, attrition is no longer an issue and instead, layoffs are the order of the day, in relatively better performing Asian countries, attrition has come back to haunt the companies. **There are many reasons for attrition and usually research has shown that the most cited reason is that the employee is unable to get on with his or her manager**. The adage that employees leave managers rather than organizations is a favorite catchphrase among management experts and organizational behavior theorists. Having said that, it must be remembered that attrition is also because of other factors like employees being unhappy with their salary or the raise that they get after the appraisal period. Further, attrition can also be because employees perceive that the current organization is not doing well and hence, they are on the lookout for better performing peers and competitors. Apart from this, attrition is also because employees find jobs in other companies that are more fulfilling and match their skill sets and profiles.

The Red Lists and Risk Management

After analyzing the reasons for attrition, it is time to look at how companies and the HR managers can manage attrition. In many organizations, managers are asked to identify potential cases of attrition before the employee actually puts in his or her papers. For instance, many multinationals have the practice of asking their managers to prepare lists of potential employees who are likely to quit. This "red list" is then sent to the managers' supervisor and the HR manager so that when the employee actually quits or even does not quit, the organization is prepared for the quitting event or counseling the employee against quitting. The latter scenario happens when the employee is deemed valuable to the organization and the manager identifies such attrition as being a loss to the company. Further, attrition is also managed by the HR department organizing periodic one-one sessions with the middle management and the managers having the same one-one session with their employees. The rationale for such sessions is that the employees would vent their frustrations or lack of comfort with the manager or with the organization and hence, ways and means can be found to address the employees' concerns.

Some Real World Case Studies

Attrition has become a challenge for companies like the Indian IT major, Infosys that has seen unprecedented attrition among its employees in recent months. The situation has deteriorated to the extent that the company is having to address investor and analyst queries about this issue and has had to come up with a plan to tackle the same. The point here is that attrition in well-known companies affects their brand value and their brand image and considering the fact that companies like Microsoft and Unilever as well as P&G are respected globally for their HR practices, attrition in these companies dents the carefully crafted image of being people friendly. This is the reason why the blue chip companies take attrition seriously and to the point where Steve Balmer (the former head of Microsoft) is reported to have gone through all the exit interview forms of the employees.

Concluding Thoughts

Finally, attrition is also economically damaging to the organizations as the replacement employees have to be hired at a cost and trained again at a cost. Further, losing employees who are well versed with the organizational culture can mean a loss of valuable resources that lead to a situation where the organization stands to miss the potential value adding activities of the employees. It is for this reason that HR managers and organizations take attrition seriously and consider ways and means to curb the same.

www.ingramcontent.com/pod-product-compliance
Lightning Source LLC
Chambersburg PA
CBHW080824180526
45168CB00006B/2564